Puff Up, Pufferfish!

Written by Michèle Dufresne

PIONEER VALLEY EDUCATIONAL PRESS, INC.

Here is a **pufferfish**.
Like most fish,
pufferfish have gills.

gill
Gills help fish breathe.

To escape predators, the pufferfish swallows lots of water and makes itself so large and round that it cannot be eaten.

A pufferfish has **poison**.
It can kill a **predator**.

A pufferfish has toxins in its body that make it poisonous to eat.

Yum! Yum!
The pufferfish sees a clam!
A big pufferfish can crack
the clam's shell.
Pufferfish have four teeth that act like a beak to open and eat all kinds of shellfish.
8

Here is a grass puffer.

The grass puffer can

put out a smell.

Scientists believe grass puffers put out
a smell that attracts other grass puffers.

Grass puffers live in Asia. Some people keep grass puffers as pets.

glossary

pufferfish

water

poison

predator